Stories
from the
Amazon

by
Saviour Pirotta

Illustrated by
Becky Gryspeerdt

RSVP
RAINTREE
STECK-VAUGHN
PUBLISHERS
A Steck-Vaughn Company

Austin, Texas
www.steck-vaughn.com

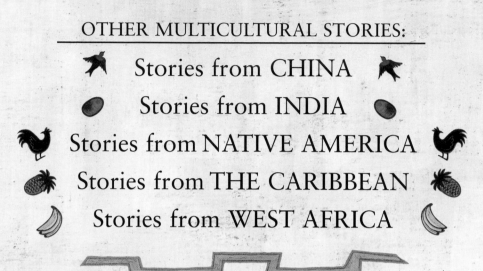

OTHER MULTICULTURAL STORIES:

Stories from CHINA

Stories from INDIA

Stories from NATIVE AMERICA

Stories from THE CARIBBEAN

Stories from WEST AFRICA

© Copyright 2000, text, Steck-Vaughn Company

Published by Raintree Steck-Vaughn Publishers,
an imprint of Steck-Vaughn Company

Library of Congress Cataloging-in-Publication Data
Pirotta, Saviour.
Stories from the Amazon / Saviour Pirotta.
p.   cm.—(Multicultural Stories)
Includes bibliographical references.
ISBN 0-7398-1332-3 (hard)
0-7398-1818-X (soft)
1. Amazon—Juvenile literature.
[1. Amazon.]
I. Title. II. Series.

Printed in Italy. Bound in the United States.
1 2 3 4 5 6 7 8 9 0 04 03 02 01 00

Contents

Introduction

Like many other people, I became interested in the Amazon rain forest when its destruction was first highlighted by the media a few years ago. Before that I had only been vaguely aware of it. I knew jaguars lived there, and vampire bats. But I never really thought much about it or its value to our planet.

Then I saw a television program about mining for gold in the Amazon River. I was horrified by the images of thoughtless destruction. Rivers were being polluted. Plants, fish, and animals were being pushed to the brink of extinction. And that wasn't all. Farmers were destroying the forest to make way for farmland. The tribal people who lived there were losing their homes. The world was losing one of its richest assets.

When you are on the verge of losing something, you immediately become aware of how precious it is. Suddenly I found myself reading avidly about rain forests in general and the Amazon in particular. I found out some incredible facts: at 1.5 million sq. mi. (4 million sq. km), the Amazon is the biggest rain forest in the world. The Amazon River is more than 4,000 miles (6,500 km) long and is home to 2,500 species of fish. Countless animals, insects, and plants, many of which we don't know much about, live in the land around it.

This book and its stories are a celebration of the Amazon rain forest and its peoples, cultures, and treasures. I hope it will make many of you aware how wonderful it is and how important it is to save before it is lost.

Saviour Pirotta

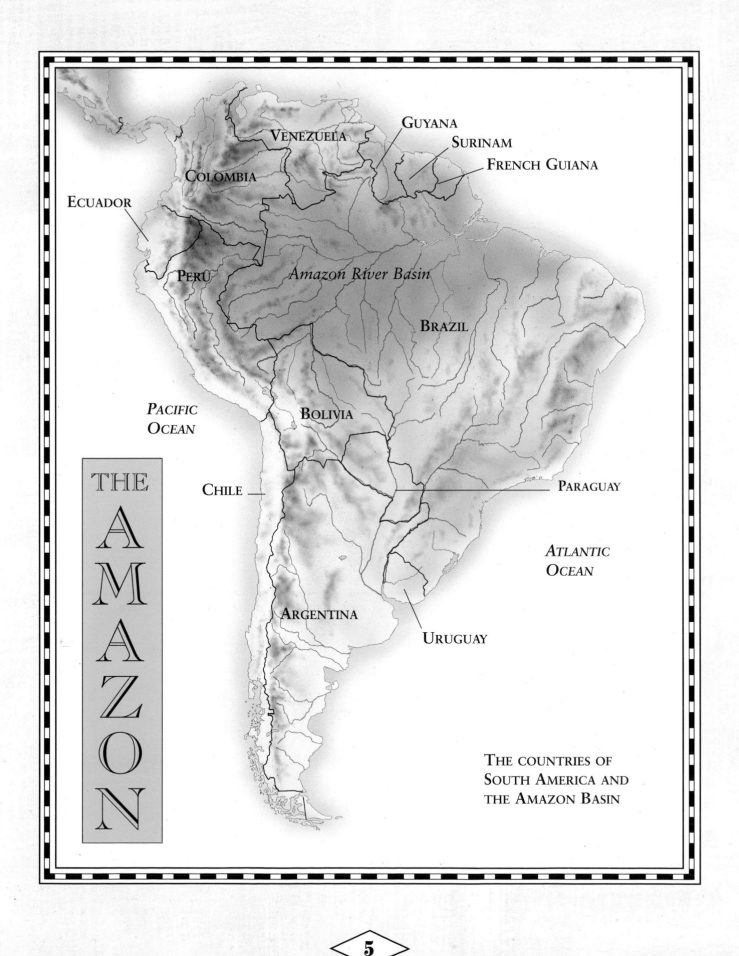

THE AMAZON

GUYANA

VENEZUELA

SURINAM

FRENCH GUIANA

COLOMBIA

ECUADOR

PERU

Amazon River Basin

BRAZIL

Pacific Ocean

BOLIVIA

CHILE — — PARAGUAY

Atlantic Ocean

ARGENTINA

URUGUAY

THE COUNTRIES OF
SOUTH AMERICA AND
THE AMAZON BASIN

HOW THE WORLD BEGAN

Almost all peoples try to explain the creation of the world around them through myths and legends. We also use stories to show how gods brought order out of chaos, how the first people came to the world, and how they learned the first tasks of civilization.

The peoples of the Amazon have many creation myths. The Yanomami tell of Omam, a birdlike god who created the world, the forest, and all the plants and living creatures in it. Meanwhile, the Trio people of Brazil have a story about Waraku. She was the spirit of a fish, who taught a fisherman named Paraparawa how to grow yams and potatoes, how to make tools and utensils, and how to cook food and make bread.

Region in which the Kamayura live

XINGU PARK

BRAZIL

MATO GROSSO

The creation story that starts on the next page is told by the Kamayura people, who live in the forests of Brazil.

This region is in the northeast of Brazil, near the mouth of the Amazon.

The Legend of the Sun God

In the beginning there was no light in the forest. All the sun's golden rays were caught up in the Kingdom of the Birds, high above the trees. The people woke up in the dark and went to bed in the dark. They could never see anything around them.

"This is most unfair," said Kuat, the sun god. "I want everyone to enjoy the light."

"It's that Urubutsin, the king of the vultures," sighed his brother Iae, who was the moon god. "He has knitted the tops of the trees together so that no light shines on the ground."

"Well," said Kuat, "I'm going to set things right. You just watch me."

He looked down at the world. The people were stumbling around in the darkness, banging their heads against trees and tripping over roots. "I must lure Urubutsin down there," he said. "He shall see for himself what it is like to live in darkness."

Kuat spied a dead body lying on the riverbank. Its eyes shone bright white in the dark. Something was crawling all over its decaying skin—a pile of hungry maggots.

Kuat called for the king of the flies. "Get your subjects to settle on that body," he ordered. "Tell them to make as much noise as they can."

The flies settled on the body. They flapped their wings to make as much noise as possible. Urubutsin, who was sitting in the trees, noticed them right away.

"What are those flies feasting on?" he asked.

He flew down to have a look. The flies scattered, leaving the corpse for the vulture.

Urubutsin landed on the dead man's chest. He picked out the eyes with his beak and gobbled them up. Then he started on the flesh.

"Do you like it?" asked the king of the flies.

"Yes," said Urubutsin.

"It's a present from Kuat, the sun god," said the king of the flies. "Tomorrow he might send you another one."

"In that case," said Urubutsin, "I shall be back around lunchtime." He flew off into the trees. If vultures had lips, he would have licked them.

The king of the flies reported back to Kuat. Kuat told the flies to find another body. They were to move it to the banks of the river, where Urubutsin was sure to see it.

That night, Kuat slipped through the trees down to the ground. The forest smelled damp and musty. Everything around him seemed to be festering. There were no flowers or butterflies, only mushrooms and frogs and scorpions looking for food. Kuat slipped inside the dead body and lay very still. The maggots, sensing his presence, scattered. But Kuat willed them back. The next day at lunchtime, the flies returned.

"Urubutsin is coming," said the king of the flies. The king of the vultures settled on the dead body. Again he pecked out the eyes and ate them. Then he feasted on the rotting flesh. Soon he'd eaten enough.

"I must tell my subjects about this," said Urubutsin out loud. He spread his wings to fly. But just then Kuat reached out and grabbed him by the foot. Urubutsin screamed.

"Let me go," he snarled.

"No," said Kuat, "I want you to stay here forever, where it is dark and damp."

"I am a bird," argued Urubutsin. "I was made to fly in the light."

"The people are meant to be in the light," said Kuat, "but you have condemned them to live in the dark."

The king of the vultures flapped his wings, trying to escape.

"I shall not let go," warned Kuat, "until you promise to let the sun shine down into the forest."

"I shall never do that," said Urubutsin.

"Very well, then," laughed Kuat. "Stay here in the dark forever." Urubutsin made one last attempt to escape, but he knew that Kuat was too powerful for him.

"I give in," he screeched. "Let me go, and I shall let light into the forest."

"No," said Kuat, "let the light in first."

The king of the vultures summoned his minions. "Let the light shine into the forest," he commanded. The birds flew up into the trees and ripped the branches of the trees apart with their beaks. The sun's light shone down on the forest. The people were blinded at first. Then they held their faces up to receive the sun's warmth.

And ever since then, the sun's light has shone in the forest every day.

FLOODS AND DISASTERS

It seems that every culture on Earth has a story about the world being submerged under water. In the rain forest, the Ipurina people tell of Mayuruberu, the chief of the storks. He caused a flood when he forgot that he had put his kettle on the sun to boil and it overflowed. The Tupi people believe in Monan. He made the world, but destroyed it with fire and tidal waves before rebuilding it again.

Many flood myths follow the same pattern as the story of Noah's flood in the Bible. The first people do something that angers their god. God sends a flood to wipe them out. But a handful of good people survive. They start a new, and better, world.

In the Amazon, parts of the forest flood every year. The floods destroy, but they also bring new life by spreading seeds.

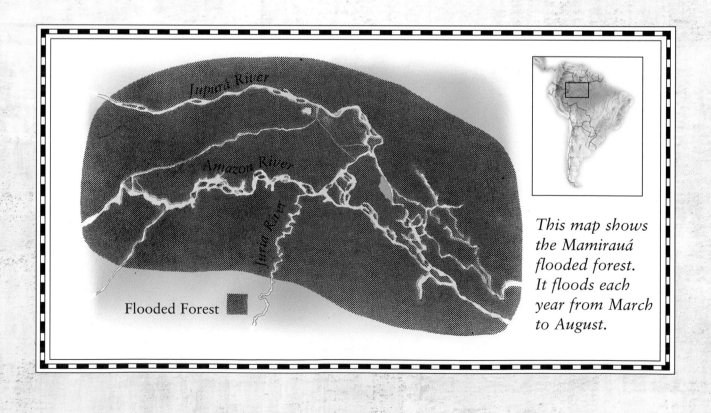

Iupurá River

Amazon River

Juriá River

Flooded Forest

This map shows the Mamirauá flooded forest. It floods each year from March to August.

The Tree of Life

Back at the start of time, the forest was a different place. All the first people had to eat were leaves or berries.

Agouti walked through the forest. He'd been searching for something delicious to eat, but yet again he hadn't found anything but leaves and berries.

No one knew how long Agouti walked, but at last he came to a part of the forest he had never seen before. He could smell something in the air, something sweet and tangy. It made his mouth water. Agouti followed his nose. He kept on walking and walking, till at last he stood in front of a great tree, with branches that seemed to reach right into the big blue sky.

"Dear me!" cried Agouti. The tree was covered with every kind of fruit you can imagine: apricots, bananas, coconuts, dates, and oranges. You name it—it was hanging there.

Agouti climbed into the branches and started eating. "I shall not tell anyone about this tree," he said. "I shall keep all this fruit for myself."

A week later Agouti's brother, who was named Macounaima, said to his friends and his other brothers: "Have you noticed how fat Agouti is growing?"

"Yes," said the others. "He must be having something more than leaves and berries to eat."

Early the next morning, Macounaima slipped out of his hammock. Agouti was already up, his belly rumbling with hunger.

"Good morning," said Macounaima.

"Morning," said Agouti. He didn't look at all pleased to see his brother.

"Going to find more berries?" asked Macounaima.

"Yes," snapped Agouti.

"I shall come with you," said Macounaima.

"I'd rather go on my own," mumbled Agouti.

"You are hiding something from me," said Macounaima. "You have found something more than leaves and berries to eat. Come on, own up."

"All right," whispered Agouti. "But if I tell what and where it is, you must promise to keep it a secret."

"I promise," said Macounaima.

Agouti led his brother to the giant tree. Macounaima's jaw dropped when he saw all the fruit. "This is the Tree of Life itself," he said. "We can't keep a thing like this to ourselves." He gathered some fruit and took it back home. All the people in the village had a taste.

"Where did you find all this?" they asked. "Tell us, so we can get some more."

"Come," said Macounaima, "I'll show you."

The entire village followed him to the Tree of Life. "Go away," said Agouti, who was sitting under the tree, eating bananas. "This is my tree."

The villagers ignored him. They started picking the ripe fruit that had fallen to the ground. The children climbed into the lower branches.

"Be careful," said Agouti, "we must leave some fruit for tomorrow."

"Nonsense," laughed the people. "The tree will bear more fruit tomorrow."

More and more children swarmed up the tree. They tore the fruit off the branches and threw it to the ground. Someone poked a wasps' nest. The wasps buzzed angrily. A boy got stung.

"That's it," said the boy's father. "Let's chop the tree down before anyone else gets hurt."

"No!" said Macounaima and Agouti together. But their voices were drowned out by the villagers' laughter. In no time at all, the mighty tree fell over.

Suddenly there was a loud roar. A deluge of icy water burst through the tree stump. Soon the whole forest was drowned. Macounaima and his people had to find shelter on a high mountain, leaving the precious fruit behind them. There they sat for many days, perishing in the heat of the sun.

When at last the water dried, Macounaima led everyone back to the forest. The Tree of Life was nowhere to be seen. But all over the forest were thousands of new trees, each one bearing one kind of fruit. They had grown out of the seeds inside the fruit scattered by the water.

THE AMAZON MIRACLE PLANT

The rain forest is filled with an incredible array of fruits and vegetables, which have sustained the forest peoples for thousands of years. One of these is Guarana.

This Guarana plant's berries are just about ripe.

Guarana was first discovered by the Maues people. They made a pulp out of it and drank it. Many farmers have tried to grow Guarana outside the rain forest, but with no success. Even today, when you can buy Guarana gum in many stores, the best crops still come from the place in which it was first found. And no Guarana grows outside of the Amazon region. The locals say it is a miracle plant. It cures headaches, upset stomachs, and sleeplessness and gives people energy when they are tired.

No wonder there are so many legends about Guarana.

Buried Eyes

The good god Tupa lived in the forest. Every day he looked after the people, making sure that the evil god Jurupari, the lord of the darkness, would not hurt them. The people could not see Tupa, but he blew with the breeze, shone with the sun, and twinkled with the stars that peeped out of the heavens. Every day the people came to him with prayers. "Good Lord Tupa," they begged, "let us find enough food to eat, keep the snakes and the jaguars away from our children, and heal our wounded hunters."

One couple, who desperately wanted a child, never asked Tupa for food or pleasant dreams. Instead they made the same request over and over again.

"Oh Good God Tupa, give us a child to look after and care for. We'll teach it to love and respect you."

Tupa looked into the couple's hearts and saw that they would make excellent parents. So he granted their wish.

Some time later the woman had a baby, a chubby little boy with a nose like a button. All the people in the tribe adored him. They brought him presents. When his mother took him down to the river, the girls all helped bathe him.

The baby grew into a strong, happy boy with big, soft eyes. He was also kind and generous. Everywhere he went, people gathered around to listen to his stories and jokes.

"He is the best hunter in the forest," said the old men when they sat together talking.

"And the best-looking one, too," sighed the girls. "He has wonderful eyes."

"He is the kindest young man we ever met," said the old women.

"And the bravest fighter," agreed the boys. "No one is ever scared when he's around."

The good god Tupa was very pleased with the boy. But the evil god Jurupari was jealous of him.

"No one thinks of me now," Jurupari moaned, lurking in the deepest, thickest shadows. "Everyone seems to have forgotten me. I am the fear, the darkness of the night. I am the maker of nightmares and the bringer of the storms.

Yet no one thinks of me anymore as they go to bed. No one shivers at the mention of my name. And it is all this boy's fault. His kindness has banished fear from the forest. I am dying because of him."

Because the gods can take any shape that they like, Jurupari turned himself into a serpent. He crawled through the bushes and sneaked into the village. There was the boy, sitting outside the longhouse, surrounded by friends and admirers.

"Tell us a joke," the children begged the boy. "Sing us a song, a funny one."

The boy laughed, and the sound of his laughter scattered around the small village like a thousand butterflies. Jurupari winced at the sound, releasing a foul stench from his mouth.

"I must get some fruit for my mother," said the boy. "But I'll tell you a story when I get back."

He picked up a basket and set
off into the forest. Jurupari followed him,
dragging his cold belly among the rotting leaves.
Soon the boy stopped to pick some berries. Jurupari
crept closer and closer, his tail twitching with evil intent.
"I shall kill the boy," he said, "then the people will
start thinking of me again." The boy started whistling.
Jurupari could see his hand tugging at one fruit after another.
The flesh was golden brown against the pale green of the leaves.
The fruit looked so clean and healthy and full of warmth that it
made Jurupati moan with envy. He sprang out of the
undergrowth and hooked his fangs into the brown flesh.
Almost instantly, the boy fell dead on the ground.
"Something's happened to my son," screamed the boy's
mother in the village. "I can feel it in my bones."

People ran to look for the boy. They found him lying on the banks of the river, the color drained from his cold flesh. His eyes were glassy, the white turned to a dull red. An old woman closed them gently with her hands.

The hunters brought the dead boy into the village and laid him outside the longhouse. Everyone sobbed, cursing the evil Jurupari for his crime. His mother kissed his cold cheeks.

"Why?" she cried. "Why would the good Tupa give me a son and then let Jurupari take him away from me?" Suddenly a thunderbolt hit the ground beside the longhouse. The woman heard a soft voice whispering in her ear. "Plant the boy's eyes in the ground," it said, "and your son shall never stop looking after you."

The woman realized that the voice belonged to Tupa. She plucked out the boy's eyes and buried them just where the thunderbolt had struck. The next day she noticed a small bush growing on the spot. Other people noticed it, too. They watered it carefully and made sure the snails did not nibble on its leaves.

The bush grew bigger and bigger, and soon red berries appeared on its branches. They were the first Guarana, the fruit that gives the forest people strength and stamina. The boy's mother picked them, and, when they popped open, she discovered large seeds inside. They stared up at her just like the eyes of her son.

THE BOAT PLANT

Many of the amazing trees and plants that grow in the rain forest can't be found anywhere else. One of the strangest is the cannonball tree. Its enormous seeds are as hard as iron, and they drop to the ground with a loud noise that sounds exactly like cannon fire. Then there's the Strangler Fig, a notorious creeper that wraps itself around a tree until it dies. The creeper then takes its victim's place in the sun.

The pads of the Vitoria Regis lily plant are so large that small animals and—some people say—even little children can float on them.

But perhaps the most awe-inspiring rain forest plant is the record-breaking Vitoria Regis. This is the biggest water lily in the world. Its lily pads are so massive that animals and small children can float across the water on them. This next story is one the rain forest people tell about the Vitoria Regis.

The Sad Song of the Moon

Late every evening, a group of young women went down to the river. They bathed in the warm water, singing beautiful love songs and telling stories. Afterward they lay on the grass and looked up at the darkening skies.

"How big are the heavens?" one of them would ask. "Who knows what wonderful mysteries hide up there?"

"I wish I were a star," another girl would sigh. "Then I could shoot across the sky and touch the rising moon."

"We all want to be stars," the rest of the girls would say. "Then we could live forever."

One night the girls stayed longer by the river than usual. The evening sky turned jet black, and the stars twinkled brighter than normal. The moon was full to bursting point with bright light, casting a silver mantle over the forest.

The girls could not believe their eyes. They had never seen such dazzling splendor before.

The night air was heavy with the scent of tropical flowers. Fireflies danced in the bushes, weaving intricate patterns of green light. The girls felt lightheaded, as if they were in a dream. The youngest of the girls, Naia, opened her arms to welcome the light of the full moon. "How I wish I could touch you," she whispered. "Then I too would be filled with your heavenly light."

The moon, hanging low in the
sky, reached out to caress Naia's face
with its silver rays. She sat up and
looked around.

"What are you looking for?" asked
one of her friends.

"A way to reach the moon," whispered Naia. "If I
touch it, it will make me a star." She stood up and
walked over to a big tree. "Come on," she called to
the others. "Follow me." The girls climbed up to the
very top of the tree. They reached out, their hands
filled with fragrant orchids. But the moon was higher
in the sky than they had expected.

"What a shame," said one of them. "Now we'll
never become stars."

The eldest led the way back to the ground. Naia
could not sleep that night. She kept thinking of the
moon and the soft silver rays that had caressed her
face. "We must try to reach it before it rises too
high," she said.

The next evening, the girls did not go down to the river. Instead, they climbed up to the top of the highest hill. When the moon rose, they reached out to touch it. But again, it was far too high for them to reach. Disappointed, the girls returned home.

"The moon is out of reach," said the eldest girl. "We should stop trying to reach it. Perhaps we are meant to be down here in the forest and not up there in the sky."

"You are right," said the other girls. "Let us forget about the moon. Let us think about the boys instead. They are real; they will love us and make us happy."

But Naia would not give up her dreams. She loved the moon too much. "I will not marry anyone," she said. "I only want the moon."

When the rest of the girls were asleep, she crept down to the river. It was a still night. There was a only a faint ripple on the surface of the water. Naia sat on the bank and looked up at the sky. The moon appeared to be brighter than usual. Its light touched every flower, every passing moth, filling their petals and wings with light.

"Oh moon, moon," sighed Naia, "I cannot come up to you. Why do you not come down to me?" Just then the breeze dropped and the river lay still. Naia saw the moon's reflection on the surface of the water.

"Hello!" she cried, thinking the moon had come down from the skies to see her. "Wait for me, I'm coming."

She got to her feet and started walking along the bank of the river. The moon's reflection, of course, moved on before her.

"Wait for me, moon," called Naia, "I cannot keep up with you." At last, she stopped walking.

Then, the moon's reflection stopped moving. It sat out in the middle of the river, where the water was dark and cold and deep. "I'm coming, moon," said Naia. She held out her hands and dived into the river. Poor Naia. The cold water made her numb, and the weeds grabbed at her feet. She struggled to get to the moon's reflection but the cold water stung her eyes and filled her mouth. Soon the current had dragged her under.

Naia's friends looked for her everywhere. But they could not find her. Instead they found a new plant, floating right in the middle of the river where Naia had drowned. It was a giant lily, pink and fragrant in the morning light. Its beautiful petals were wide open, like Naia's arms trying to catch the moon's light.

"This is the work of the moon," they said. "He has changed Naia into a water plant, so that she will always be here, ready to welcome his bright reflection on the water."

THE PINK DOLPHIN, BUOTO

VENEZUELA

Orinoco River

Amazon River

BRAZIL

The waters of the Amazon and Orinoco are home to the Pink Dolphin, known as Buoto by the local people. It is the only dolphin in the world that has a neck. Buotos usually eat small fish and soft crabs. But during the rainy season, when the Amazon floods the forest, they swim around the treetops to nibble at fruit.

The rain forest people have many legends about dolphins. Some people believe that the dolphins were once human beings who went to live in a golden city at the bottom of the river. Sometimes these magical dolphins remember the lives and friends they once had and return to land—with dire consequences for the people they meet.

Bufeo Colorado

Rosa and Paulo sat next to Grandma on the back porch. It was late in the evening, and the day's chores had been done. Laura, their elder sister, was at work, helping out in Uncle Mario's bar.

"Tell us a story, Grandma," said Paulo.

Grandma turned down the storm lamp, so they wouldn't use too much paraffin.

"What kind of story do you want?" she asked.

"A story about dolphins," replied Paulo. "Pink dolphins."

"Pink dolphins are very mysterious creatures," Grandma said. "Some people believe they were once gods who lived in a wonderful city at the bottom of the river. Now they are just dolphins, but they have strange powers all the same. They can do magic."

"What kind of magic?" asked Rosa.

"The leader of the dolphins is called Bufeo Colorado," whispered Grandma. "Sometimes he changes into a man and comes out of the water. He is always dressed smartly in a crisp linen suit. And he always wears a hat on his head. Always."

"Even when he goes to the bathroom?" asked Rosa.

Grandma nodded. "Bufeo Colorado might be able to change into a very handsome man," she said, "but he can't make the blowhole on top of his head disappear. So he hides it under a hat."

"What does he come to the forest for?" Rosa wanted to know.

"What Bufeo Colorado wants most of all," said Grandma, "is to marry a human girl. So he comes to the forest to look for a bride. Just one kiss from the handsome Bufeo and the girl falls under his spell. She follows him into the river and, once she sets eyes on the fabulous city below the waves, she forgets all about her home in the forest. She becomes a pink dolphin herself."

Rosa shuddered. "I wouldn't want to live forever at the bottom of the river," she said. "It must be very cold down there."

"That's why you must beware all men who wear straw hats," warned Grandma. "Any one of them might be Bufeo Colorado looking for a wife."

Just then Papa came out on the porch to have some dinner. "Why don't you tell the children a true story, Mama?" he asked.

"But this is a true story," said Rosa. "Isn't it, Grandma?" Grandma smiled as all storytellers do when you ask them if their stories are true. "Perhaps it is. Who knows? The world is full of unexplained mysteries." She turned up the storm lamp so Papa could see to eat his dinner.

Rosa and Paulo went to bed. But Rosa could not sleep. Did Bufeo Colorado really exist, she wondered, or had Granny just made him up?

A week later, Rosa and Paulo were fishing on the banks of the river. Suddenly there was a rustle in the bushes behind them. They both turned at once, expecting to see a capybara or a small deer emerging from the undergrowth. Instead, they saw a man in a white linen suit. He was terribly handsome. And on his head he wore a straw hat. Paulo and Rosa stiffened.

"Don't be frightened of me," said the man with a smile. "My name is Carlos. I've come to sell the local ladies some combs. Which way to the town, please?"

"Through there," said Paulo, pointing to the path they'd used to come from the village.

"No, don't go that way," interrupted Rosa. "That's a shortcut only the locals use. You might get lost in the forest. Take the path along the river. It's longer but safer."

"Thank you," said the stranger. He started walking along the riverbank, whistling a merry tune.

"That's Bufeo Colorado, isn't it?" whispered Rosa.

"It looks like him," said Paulo. "Come on, let's warn the others before he gets to town."

They dropped their fishing lines and ran along the shortcut through the bushes. When they got to the village, they burst into Uncle Mario's bar.

"There's a stranger," stammered Paulo. "He's..."

"Selling combs to the lovely ladies," said a familiar voice at one of the tables.

Rosa and Paulo turned around abruptly. The stranger was sitting on a bench, drinking tea out of a glass. Somehow he had made it to the village before them. "Thank you for showing me the way," he said. And he took off his hat to fan his face.

Paulo and Rosa stared. There was no blowhole on top of the man's head. There was only thick, black curly hair, shiny with hair oil.

"We thought you were Bufeo Colorado," said Paulo, sighing with relief.

"We thought you might put a spell on our sister Laura," added Rosa.

The stranger laughed. "I told you my name is Carlos," he said. He tossed a couple of coins on the table. "Give the children an ice cream, barman. They've been a great help."

Uncle Mario brought two ice creams to the table. The man finished his tea and stood up. "Good afternoon to you all," he said, heading for the door.

Paulo and Rosa ate their ice creams slowly, enjoying every single spoonful.

"The man's forgotten his change," said Uncle Mario when they'd finished, "Rosa, you go and give it to him. He's staying at the Hotel Splendor."

Rosa hurried along the deserted street. The Hotel Splendor was right on the other side of town. It was really a converted farmhouse, with an open-air restaurant on the roof. Rosa made her way around to the back of the building. She could hear the stranger singing along with the radio.

"Mister," she called, looking in through the window.

But the stranger did not hear her. He was standing in front of the mirror, getting ready to shave. As Rosa watched, he took off his hat. Then he took off his HAIR. Rosa realized that the shiny black curls were a wig. The stranger was completely bald. And in the middle of his head he had—a blowhole.

Glossary

Agouti A ratlike creature that lives in the forests and grasslands of South America. It has very strong legs that make it very agile. The boy in our story was called Agouti because he could walk for hours on end without getting tired.

Canopy A sort of platform formed by the branches of rain forest trees growing into each other. It is home to thousands of plants and living creatures, but it also keeps sunlight from getting through to the forest floor.

Capybara a member of the rat family that lives on the riverbanks of the rain forest. It looks like a giant guinea pig and can swim.

Fireflies Small insects found in warm climates. Chemicals in parts of their bodies enable them to glow in the dark.

Jaguar A ferocious member of the cat family. It is the largest predator in the rain forest, although it rarely attacks people. The people of the Amazon have great respect for the jaguar. Some dress in jaguar pelts for special ceremonies. Others paint jaguar patterns on their faces.

Macounaima In Amazon folklore, Macounaima is a trickster and a hero. As a child, he was very lazy and got into a lot of trouble. But people liked his nerve and courage.

Maggots Small, wormlike creatures that turn into flies. They have no legs and live in rotting meat.

Vultures Huge birds that feed on dead meat. They have large wings that help them soar while looking for food. Vultures can tell when a wounded person or animal is going to die, so the birds hang around, waiting for their dinner.

Books to Read

Green, Jen. *Learn About Rain Forests* (Learn About). New York: Lorenz Books, 1998.

Goodman, Susan E. *Bats, Bugs, and Biodiversity: Adventures in the Amazonian Rain Forest.* New York: Atheneum Books for Young Readers, 1995.

Lewington, Anna. *Atlas of the Rain Forests.* Austin, TX: Raintree Steck-Vaughn, 1997.

Mason, Paul, editor. *Atlas of Threatened Cultures.* Austin, TX: Raintree Steck-Vaughn, 1997.

Patent, Dorothy Hinshaw. *Children Save the Rain Forest.* New York: Penguin Putnam, 1996.

Riley, Peter D., et al. *Nightwatch: Nightlife in the Tropical Rain Forest* (Windows on Science). Pleasantville, NY: Reader's Digest, 1999.

Ross, Kathy. *Crafts for Kids Who Are Wild About Rainforests* (Crafts for Kids Who Are Wild About). Brookfield, CT: Millbrook, 1997.

Theodorou, Rod. *Up a Rain Forest Tree* (Amazing Journeys). Portsmouth, NH: Heinemann Library, 1998.

Rain Forest Activities

Communal dancing is a very important part of rain forest life. Create a dance drama telling the **Legend of the Sun God**, which is full of flowing movement. The leading dancers could play Kuat, Urubutsin, and Iae. The rest of the class can be the chorus. Their job is to portray the birds, worms, and flies. Everyone could wear a mask to show who they are. Alternatively, they could paint patterns and symbols on their faces.

Make your own **Tree of Life**. Cut out a tree shape, and then pin it up on the wall. Invite everyone to bring in pictures of fruit cut out of old magazines. How many different kinds of fruits from the rain forest can you paste on the tree?

Flood stories like **The Tree of Life** are very popular all around the world. Imagine there is a flood in your school, then make up a play about it. You could borrow ideas from various flood stories.

Buried Eyes and **The Sad Song of the Moon** are two stories that explain the origins of fruits and plants. Make up your own tales about fruit bought from your local supermarket. The stories could then be made into a book.

Get your class to write reports about sightings of **Bufeo Colorado.** The reports could be collected into a newsletter. Alternatively, make a news report on video. "Reporters" could speak to the camera and interview "eyewitnesses."

Underwater cities have captured the imagination of many writers. Write your own stories about a city at the bottom of the Amazon. Its inhabitants could be some of the characters and animals featured in this book.